A

MW01103804

to

Householders

CENTRAL CHINMAYA MISSION TRUST

© **Central Chinmaya Mission Trust**

Originally Printed in U.S.A.
Printed in India   Dec.2001 to Dec.2010   15,000 copies
Reprint   February   2012   2,000 copies

Published by :
CENTRAL CHINMAYA MISSION TRUST
Sandeepany Sadhanalaya,
Saki Vihar Road,
Mumbai   400 072, India
Tel. : (91-22) 2857 2367 / 2857 5806
Fax : (91-22) 2857 3065
E-mail : ccmtpublications@chinmayamission.com
Website : www.chinmayamission.com

Distribution Centre in USA :
CHINMAYA MISSION WEST
Publications Division,
560 Bridgetown Pike,
Langhorne, PA 19053, USA.
Phone : (215) 396-0390
Fax : (215) 396-9710
Email : publications@chinmayamission.org
Website : www.chinmayapublications.org

Printed by :
PRIYA GRAPHICS
Unit No. J - 120, Ansa Industrial Estate,
Saki Vihar Road, Sakinaka, (Andheri)
Mumbai - 400 072. (India)
Tel. No. 6695 9935 / 4005 9936
Email: chinmayapriya@hotmail.com

Price : Rs : 30=00

ISBN: 978-81-7597-025-0

Contents

Guidance from the Guru
Swami Tapovanam

[Following are the contents of some of the letters
that Swami Tapovanam wrote in 1950 to a devout
couple who lived in South India.]

**A householder's life is mainly one of action and
those in that stage of life ought to do their best
to keep their actions pure-**

*Take a vow not to do anything impure or forbidden
by the scriptures even to save your life .*Use our
wisdom to perform every action as an act of divine
worship without caring for its results. Thus make all
actions pure, uncontaminated by the desire for
reward. This should be the first spiritual practice of
every aspirant. To achieve this, control over the
senses and the mind is absolutely essential. Purity
of action is the very foundation of all spiritual
exercises. If one cannot perform good deeds, then
how can one aspire for the far loftier steps of
devotion to God and realization of Brahman ?

*To worship a chosen deity is not only easier, it is
also more suited to the times.* One can worship
one's chosen deity with good deeds and moral
conduct. Repeat the *mantra*-s of the deity, worship
His image, meditate upon Him. By such acts of
devotion and by the performance of good deeds (of
course, without desiring their results) one ought to
purify and concentrate one's mind. Only a mind
shorn of all impurities of likes and dislikes becomes
entitled to follow the path of Self-inquiry. The

sole means of liberation is the immediate knowledge of Self, arising out of the inquiry of the Self. That is the goal which we have to reach step by step.

The practice of breath control (praanaayaama) is not indispensable. To a mind that naturally finds pleasure in repetition of a *mantra japa* and meditation (*dhyaana*), it is practically of little use. It is when an aspirant's mind proves unamenable to control, remains wavering and unsteady, prone to rush outward at the least provocation, that *praanaayaama* and similar practices of *hatha yoga* are prescribed to control the mind. Therefore, give up thoughts of the kind. Practice one steady sitting posture and engage yourself in devotional practices.

Remember God at all times. It is no spiritual life to spend a few minutes in the morning and evening thinking of God and devote the rest of the time to thoughts of sensuous pleasures. Think of the Lord in the midst of work and never for a moment forget Him.

Balance of Mind

Concentrate your mind upon japa and meditation. As a rule, in the early morning and night, sit in a firm posture for as long as possible and go on repeating the names of God. Also meditate upon His form. In the early stages, the mind will be prone to stray, but do not give up. If one has sincere faith in God and love for Him, these exercises can only produce joy.

Moderation in conversation is a great spiritual practice. As far as possible think and talk of God. Do not pollute your mind with trivial conversation and avoid criticism of others. Do not spend much time listening to news or reading newspapers, and above all avoid bad company as it will disturb the mind. Occasionally observe a day of silence. Eat only pure (*sattvic*) food. Never eat too much, as excessive and impure food can put the aspirant in difficulties. On some days it is good to restrict the diet to fruit alone, or to fast completely in conjunction with the silent worship of God.*Reading books of devotion and Self-knowledge,* and consideration of their purport for an hour or two daily, will help to lift the mind above worldly affairs and strengthen the spirit of dis-passion. Association with mahatmas is still more beneficial. No book, no scripture, can confer the same degree of benefit.. But real renunciates (*sadhu*-s) are, of course, rare, and chances to associate with them are still rarer in these days. Consequently, a study of the works of ancient holy persons can be a substitute for personal contact. What else can be done?   Try to raise the mind above such pairs of opposites as pleasure and pain, friend and foe, honor and dishonor.

Maintain equanimity. But all this is possible--the mind will rise above all these--only if the goal is Godhead, nothing else. If the mind plunges into the thought of God and is immersed in it, when will it have the time and opportunity to think of such things as honor and dishonor. Balance of mind is libe-ration (*moksha*). It is God-realization. It is all transcending peace, and all transcending bliss; it is the supreme object of human life. All spiritual practices aim at this. *Perpetual delight of the mind in the God Principle is its real balance.*

Selfless Actions

One must perform one's duties, not for the sake of sensuous pleasure, but out of devotion to God. The scriptures as well as experience indicate that desire is at the root of all action. No desires, no action. If one has absolutely no desires, why should he stir out of his seat? One desires physical cleanliness, so he bathes. One desires to satisfy his hunger, so he eats. A devotee performs his actions out of love for God, as an act of service to Him. God fills the world. The world is His form. Thus, whatever is done in the world, and for the world, is an act of service to God. The devotee performs his duties out of love for the world which is His form and thus worships Him. He does nothing to enjoy the world of senses or to glorify himself. It is a worldly person who labors night and day to enjoy sense objects.

Until the mind becomes perfectly tranquil and transcends all doubt, it will not be free from desire. Desires will continue until then, either for good or for evil. Worship of God is a good action, done out of a good desire. As one worships God with flowers and japa, another who follows the path of service worships Him with good actions. His aim is to win the grace of God and reach His presence. This is the ultimate gain. In His eyes, therefore, there is no distinction between a great and small action. Through whatever God has bidden him to perform, whether it is big or small, he worships Him. *This is an important truth a householder ought to know.*

The absence or presence of selfishness determines whether the action is good or bad. Selfishness causes an action to be sinful and impure. One cannot be affected by success or failure if selfish considerations or motives are absent from one's action.

- *Eliminate all selfish thoughts that defile the mind;*
- *Make the mind still and fix it upon the feet of God;*
- *Sit in a steady posture as long as possible and worship Him regularly*

Like a child, live in the present without worry about the past or the future; be convinced by proper thought that it is peace of mind that is the highest pleasure. That kind of life is truly spiritual, blessed, and blissful; it is coveted even by gods. There are steps still higher than these. Daily and intense steady practice enables an aspirant to ascend them.

Dispassion

A householder should not conduct himself like a recluse (vaanaprastha) or a renunciate (samn-yaasin); nor should a recluse or a renunciate behave like a householder. This is one of the important injunctions of the scriptures. A house-holder should perform all the duties pertaining to his station in life; it is not for him to live like a renunciate, nor is it desirable to do so. A house-holder, wise and dispassionate, discharges his duties not out of any desire to enjoy sense objects, but out of a conviction that it is his duty to

5

do so. He accommodates sense objects only as far as they serve to fulfill his duties and not for selfish enjoyment. To all outward appearances, there may be no difference between him and a purely worldly person; both perform their duties, but their attitudes reveal an ocean of difference.

Without dispassion there can be no knowledge of the Self. But dispassion and renunciation are entirely different. A householder may have firm dispassion; he may have no desire at all for sense enjoyment; yet, he will have to accept sense objects as a householder. A renunciate may succeed in doing his duty (uninterrupted contemplation of Brahman) without touching a coin, but a householder cannot do so. *Vairaagya* (dispassion) means having no *raaga* (desire) within; rejecting things externally also, out of dispassion, is called renunciation. A householder may lead the life of a great *vairaagi* and great *jnaani*; but he cannot become a great *tyaagi* (renunciate) as he cannot renounce all objects because he has yet to attend to his duties as a householder. Yet he may live with self-control and happiness. What I mean to impress is this: a householder ought to perform his household duties, as service to God. For him it is indispensable to receive sense objects and deal variously with them. That agitation should result at times from this is inevitable. By nature, agitation is sorrow, and sorrow is the result of *praarabdha*. Yet for those who recognize agitation and sorrow as a form of Brahman, it will be possible to find happiness even in the midst of suffering--on a hot day, if a person stands waist-deep in cold water, he

6

experiences the heat from his head to his waist, but below the waist he feels the cold--in the same way.

If a householder becomes a person of wisdom, he should continue to perform all actions prescribed by the scriptures with or without desire for their fruit. The spiritual aspirant does his duty without desire for its fruit; thereby he purifies his mind and becomes fit for spiritual contemplation and knowledge of Self.   I hope from what I have written so far, my ideas of dispassion and renunciation sought to be conveyed in my previous letter have become still more clear. That long letter you have sent over here reveals a clean mind that loves no sensuous objects and has absolutely no liking for actions which produce agitation--a mind that longs after unbroken, divine peace. Truly such a mind is the mature result of meritorious deeds accumulated through many generations. One may maintain his life on leaves or water, sleep on bare ground, and lead a life of hard penance with absolutely no sensuous enjoyments--that is all good. But what the scriptures advise is that a householder should not abandon his household duties.

Renunciation of sensuous objects is one thing; renunciation of action is another. For fear of the scriptures, the ignorant person continues to perform his duties, but the *jnaani-* s do so, induced by the tendencies inherited from the past. Rise above all thoughts that I am the body--accept *sannyaasa*--till then action does not leave you.

Attachment to sensuous objects (rasa) arises out of the ignorance of the blissful Self, from attachment comes desire and sensuous enjoyment. The Bhagavad Geeta states that if desire must be destroyed along with attachment which is its root cause, ignorance must be annihilated through the knowledge of Truth. Aspirants may also obtain dispassion. Though their attachment and its cause, ignorance, may not have been completely eliminated, they escape from their attachment and become dispassionate by finding evil in sense objects. The evil referred to is the transitoriness and painfulness of worldly objects. Attachment persists, but through steady discrimination of the perception of evil, there is no possibility for desire to arise. If a poisonous snake or a scorpion in a hole is destroyed, everything becomes safe and secure. But one may not have the daring or the skill to attack and kill it. Even then, one will not love or touch it because of one's perception that it is poisonous and is the source of pain and suffering. Similarly, aspirants may still have lingering desires for sense enjoyments, being victims of ignorance, yet they may safeguard their dispassion through the perception of evil.

Realization of Brahman through the contemplation of Brahman is adjudged only to those aspirants who have dispassion. Without dispassion, how can an aspirant's mind engage itself in the worship of Brahman? However, that does not mean that knowers of Truth alone possess dispassion; those who find evil in sense enjoyments will also have it. It is this dispassion that is designated by Vedantins as the fourfold spiritual wealth (*saadhana chatustaya*), the means helpful to the contemplation of Brahman: discrimination (*viveka*), dispassion (*vairaagya*), control of the mind, body, and so on (*shamaadi-shatka*), faith, and desire for final liberation (*mumukshutva*). So may I repeat here that the more one practices renunciation of sense objects, the more laudable the effort is; nothing has been said previously to the effect that it is impossible for a householder to renounce sense enjoyments

- *A life of penance is good for both the householder and the renunciate.*
- *Keep away from the hustle and bustle of worldly life*
- *Exert yourself to the utmost in practicing penance and in the worship of God*

-these are good for anyone in any stage of life.

Self-Effort

Even as satisfaction of hunger is the perceptible result of eating, cheerfulness of mind and a sense of peace are the tangible result of devout worship. With regular, uninterrupted practice of worship, cleanness of mind and the feeling of peace will steadily increase. That miserable state in which common, paltry things upset the mind will cease. As a result of the unbroken contemplation of Self, sparks of Self-realization begin to flit about in the mind like flashes of lightning. Along with it, a great feeling of joy pervades the mind. Sense objects and sensuousness can no longer tempt or attract the mind. However, in the early stages of spiritual practice, aspirants must guard against sense objects and those seeking them, as they agitate the mind.

"Grace of Self, grace of God, grace of the guru, and grace of the scriptures--those who have gained these four realize truth and rejoice beyond the shadow of fear"--this is a common saying of saints. Of these, grace of Self means self-effort. God helps those who help themselves. By the grace of God, an aspirant comes into contact with a guru who is established in Brahman. And through the grace of the guru, he earns the secrets and puts them into practice. Thus he reaches the state of God-realization. So at the root of all gain is self-effort. Devote your days and nights to spiritual exercises. You will, in the end, be crowned with success. I do not propose to write much as there is no need to. Writing and reading are not very helpful toward Self-realization. They are merely diversions of the mind. Briefly know what you ought to know and then put into practice what you have learned, all with devout attention. This is what spiritual aspirants ought to do.

- *Meditate more than you read. Meditation strengthens one's resolve.*
- *Follow up resolution with action.*
- *Those who meditate more upon a subject receive more courage and strength in fulfilling their intention.*

God Alone

The first step in spiritual life is to believe firmly that God alone is true, indestructible, and blissful. Those who have such firm belief will have no attachment to sense objects and desire to enjoy them. People occupy themselves with work, if not for sense enjoyment, at least for self-glorification: "I am very rich," "I am a great leader," "I am a great scholar," "I am a great devotee." Thus people pride themselves and find a fleeting pleasure in the proud fancy. Even great persons who have given up all sorts of sense enjoyments sometimes forget their future goal, being misled by such fancy. The pleasure of utilization and pleasure of self-glorification both soon end in overwhelming sorrow. The godly pleasure originating in the contemplation of God alone is eternal; it is untouched by sorrow. The wise who know this find lasting, unbroken joy in the contemplation of God, finding no joy in anything else. By the contemplation of God, not only the individual, but the whole world becomes pure and holy.

A believer can render no greater service to the world than that rendered by the contemplation of God. That means every other service is inferior by comparison. Therefore without wasting a precious moment, without a single moment's break, perform spiritual practices to gain remembrance of God. The practice of devotion to Krishna is very good. At the beginning of spiritual life, one should prefer the practice of devotion to the practice of knowledge, because it is simpler and easier. Even for those whose discrimination and dispassion are not well established, it will not be difficult to follow devotion. Therefore repeat the Krishna *mantra* always, meditate upon His form, listen to the stories of His great qualities and powers. By following these acts of devotion regularly, try to develop divine love.

Samsaara (worldliness) is none other than the evils of the mind such as desire and anger. Once these are destroyed, there is no *samsaara* at all. He who has freed himself from *samsaara* is said to be liberated. He is now of the form of Brahman. It is to combat those evils that people resort to spiritual practices. So, at the beginning of practice, there is no point in complaining about them. If one is able to bring undesirable and unrestrained desire, anger, and so on under control, it is itself a great success. It is no sin for householders to experience, within limit, desires and anger. But for aspirants engaged in spiritual practices, the more these are restrained, the better it will be for their spiritual exercises and experiences. Indeed these are terrible obstacles in their way. If through association with holy persons, prayer, and hearing of holy stories, one is able to find delight in the thought of God, opportunities for the return of desires and anger will be minimized.

Vedanta in Action for Householders
Swami Chinmayananda

(The following article summarizes Pujya Gurudev Swami Chinmayananda's teaching to householders- the way we should live our life. These are chosen from various letters written by Swamiji to his devotees at different occasions).

Our duties

To perform and fulfill your duties correctly you must very carefully examine , reflect upon and understand life in society and your place in it. As an individual you have duties towards yourself, as a domestic being, you have duties towards your elders and to those who are younger than you,. as a social being you have duties towards the society : and lastly as a living member in a competitive world you have some duties towards yours chosen profession. All these duties are to be undertaken and fulfilled with a sense of loyalty and devotion to the Lord, who in His Great Wisdom has placed you where you are in your exact circumstances.

Our present joy is - someone's past sacrifice

Duties towards the elders, are not only at home ,but towards all elder-citizen around you. The present is the product of the past. The elder-citizen generation carved out for us our present, ill or well. We serve them in their old age, when they, tired and fatigued, sit back to rest and revive. If everyone looks after and cares for his elders and little growing children, the society blooms happy, and grows up vigorous and secure. But this is not done , because of the indifference born out of our own dirty and ugly selfishness. In our blind hunt for our personal happiness in society we ignore and refuse this duty. Thereby the neglected society groans in man-made pains. Children get neglected. Youth come to run wild, with no clear goal in life. Confusion rampant in every bosom. Morality is stampeded under foot and maimed. Corruption raises its head everywhere: within the heart of people, and in the outer world around them.

Your children - your future

Fulfill your duties towards your children by providing them with a healthy, happy environment. Start teaching them about spirituality and noble values at an early age- before the age of three. Do not ever understand that children of that age are merely passive observers. In fact, only after we have grown up do we learn the art of passive, dull, sleepy , and sloppy observation . If children of that age are passive observers, how then are they able to learn a language? Is not everything new, fresh , mysterious to them? In fact , child psychologists have concluded that children in that age group need more rest as well as more frequent feeding because during those few years of early childhood they have to be alert and learn more than in their later life. The rate of absorption of knowledge and experiences in those years is stupendous. Therefore, an atmosphere of religion and spiritual values around

them is very important in molding and enhancing
their mental life.

Between the age of three and five , your children
can be introduced to stories of Christ and Krishna,
of Rama and Buddha, of Mohammed and Moses.
These stories of the spiritual giants of the world,
recounting their experiences, their trials and inner
strength in overcoming temptations, as well as the
positive experiences of joy that they gained, may all
be passed on to your children with appropriate
expressiveness. Let these stories be told now and
then by the father also. Make it a point for the
children to pray before their meals, not too
elaborately, but for a short yet serious moment.
Whenever they ask questions about flowers, clouds,
butterflies, or frogs, be alert to flavor your honest
explanations with a hint about the play of God
around us. Leave them with these small hints ; do
not go into details. Let there be a corner in your
home for prayer - a quiet private chapel or simple
altar . Let children watch both of you praying to the
Lord regularly. When children have grown to be
between the ages of eight and ten , at a fixed time
for one half hour everyday , sit down with them and
read for them -The Gospel of Sri Ramakrishna. I
suggest this book because in it much is expressed
in the innocent language of children. The endless
stories and analogies can lead their minds on an
independent journey to see for themselves a greater
message for life and a larger value in life.

Restructure your identification

There is a duty towards yourself. You want to be a good and faithful member of the family as well as the community and the nation. How can that happen if one has not sublimated one's ego , one's sense of individuality , and has not drowned oneself in total identification with the family , community, or nation? If one still has a powerful ego , and therefore is prone to selfishness, one will only cheat the family, loot the community, and betray the nation. To belong to a group is to submerge your individuality in the group personality. What we do today is to act in the world centered in our own selfishness, our own little egos. Let us sublimate the ego and discover our identity with the holy Presence that permeates the entire universe. In the resultant sense of joyousness and fulfillment, when we then act in the world, our actions will have a creative splendor and a paternal affection. Service to other will be escalated to a benediction.

The path is the same whether one is a householder or a renunciate. As long as our attention is with the flesh, we discover a hundred excuses to run out in to the world of objects , seeking gratification. But when the mind becomes attached to an inspiring goal or ideal, its nature changes and its attention turns towards the higher . When your child is playing with your new silver-plated pen , the only way to persuade the child to give it up is to offer him a piece of chocolate candy.

Spiritual life of a householder

In a householder's life, total abstinence is not allowed. But overindulgence, all excesses such as overeating, overworking, over-anxiety ,over- ambition, must be curtailed, including over-exerting and oversleeping. Prayer in the morning and in the evening and daily reading of at least a few pages of inspiring spiritual literature should be a helpful program for both husband and wife. If you still find your mind difficult to control on a given day, take only fruit that day, but do not make it a habit, and take to this diet only when you feel that your mind is out of control.

How is a householder lady to begin a Divine Life? Read good books- study thoroughly in spare time and then think over what you have read . Do housekeeping. Spend half an hour in the morning and evening and fifteen minutes in the noon in your Pooja room for meditation. In all your spare time chant OM- OM- OM *Mahaa Mrthyunjaya mantra*. Do not indulge in the usual scandal mongering and thus waste time. See the goodness in all, ignore their faults. Keep cheerful in mind. Teach the mind to smile forth in joy. In a smiling, joyous mind Divinity seeks its shelter. Do not be over anxious for anything in life. Keep the surrender- attitude. Be regular; be regular. This is the Goal. Slowly try.

Morality - the backbone of Spiritual life

To perform your duties and to discover a joy in this very performance; to live moral values and to eliminate "likes and dislikes" in life for things and beings ; to increase your excellence in the performance of your chosen profession; all these need the basic devotion to the Lord , who has provided you with body-mind -intellect-equipment and who is the sole enlivener for all their activities. You can not perform your duties well , nor live a moral life of self - restraint and self - denial, nor step up the beauty of your professional performance, if your ego and selfish desire are not curbed and conquered fully . It is this unholy wedlock of 'I' and 'I want', that breed the many monster- children who destroy your inner spiritual peace and joy. Prayer and surrender of 'I' and 'I want' ideas at His feet in devotion are the only means. Where these two are not there the individual comes to shine in his. brilliant efficiency, in the outer world, and in his moral glow, in his inner life.

Moral values have a positive dynamism all of their own . They are not a mere negative "don't do", set of rules . They are dynamic set of positive ideas accepted in your understanding and lived with Rama-like heroism Krishna-like inner grit. Without the ability to give up , total sacrifice, of all that you have understood to be base, low and vicious , moral values cannot be fruitfully lived. We have our mightiest power in life in our intellectual faculty . This power falls under two categories: the 'conserving-power' and the 'directing-power'. Generally in life we find all successful people have developed their 'conserving-power', to varying degrees. Hence they all have different heights of success and glory gained in their life's pursuit. One may acquire a lot of wealth, or supreme political power. We must congratulate them. But if they have not discovered and diligently cultivated their 'directing-power', they will not be able to enjoy what they have gathered with their 'conserving-power'. They hoard wealth but are pestered with their fears, worries, sense of insecurity, and anxieties. They earned their wealth, power, fame and respect in the society, but in themselves they are rendered incapable of enjoying what they have, if they have not the 'directing- power'. Example of this silent inner tragedy lived by the many are everywhere for those who have eyes to see. This 'directing- power' of the intellect can be cultivated when one insists on living the moral values.

A morally well- established person entertains himself with life as Rama lived, while one who has no moral values to respect, like Ravana , may have everything in life , yet suffer and meet only an inglorious end. Thus Ramayana , in a vivid story form, clearly demonstrate not only the brilliant charm of living in the enduring moral values but also how one's life can become a dark and dreary tragedy if in spite of one's prosperous wealth and glory, might and power, one has not cultivated moral-values to live and enjoy one's life.

Game of meeting the challenges

Life is spent in 'meeting challenges'. Situations and problems, continuously flow towards us and no one need search for them. To meet them efficiently is the game. Sometime you win- sometime you loose. Meet them, we must: there is no choice. If you meet them with courage and faith in yourself, you win; if you neglect to be dynamic and diligent all the time, they will with merciless aggressiveness roll on and crush you in their blind fury. This is the law-of-life. Meet them, we must. You may win here, and may loose there. It becomes a sport, exhausting but exhilarating, no doubt, and one can enjoy it all if it is taken as a life-long sport.

In order to be on the field of life's-sport you must have a mind full of reserve energy and inexhaustible inner stamina. An exhausted and fatigued sick-mind gets hit by situation,crushed by problems, mercilessly tortured by a powerful and tyrannical life. This is not because the outer life has the strength to persecute you, but you are too weak and so allow life to play havoc upon you.

Be strong - not merely a physical strength of a bull- but the subtle vitality of a calm mind, diligent in its application , consistent in its logical thinking , replete with a will to win over all negative tendencies that poison and weaken the mind. 'Be yourself is the simple motto of Right Living. Weaknesses are not yours-rise above them. Above the level of both the good and the bad, illuminating both equally and not getting in any way contaminated by either [like the sun lighting up both the dirt and the cleanliness] reins Supreme *guha*. the Inner Essence "That Thou Art." This inner Ruling Factor is God. This Essence of life is the True You. All the sorrow and pains, losses and gains belong to the body and not the True You. You are Muruga, the *Atman* of the Vedantin.

Act, We must

Live in the Self. Know the Self. 'Be yourself.' Act in
the world without a thought for a anxiety for the fruit-
this is *Nishkaama Karma*. This is not 'stupid' as you
think , this is the most intelligent way of action. If our
actions were to yield for us its permanent and
greater wealth, this alone is the way. To 'act' in
order to gain a wished-for result is a loss in two
ways:

(a) If we gain only that which is wished for and
   nothing more; and what we wish for may be
   something too fleeting, meager and senseless. A
   boy may wish for toy, a young man for a girl, a
   mature and ambitious one may demand an
   empire. But as the toy is brittle, so to is the thrill
   of winning the darling or an empire.

(b) We may not gain the particular fruit wished for,
   and so the sorrow would be too poignant in
   proportion to the intensity with which we have
   desired for the not-got fruit.

Thus the most intelligent thing is to Act as the
occasion demands, always truthfully, honestly,
straight-forwardly without ego , vanity or boast-
fulness. Meekly, as the servant of the Great Master
act. Act because we are His servants, and the
action is only in the accomplishment of His plan.
The greater our surrender unto His will, the greater
our intensity of devotion for Him, the more constant
our mental remembrance of Him, the surer we shall
be acting parallel to His will. And His will ever works
itself out to a success.

Nishkaama Karma Yoga is the greatest path, the easiest for all devotees who have a vein of ' activity' in their composition. Act: but act ever-as a *Yagna* in total surrender to Muruga.

Secret of richness

The secret of getting is GIVE-GIVE- GIVE . Worldly people of small crumpled hearts can never understand it and modern economics has not dared to expound it. Give away the last penny and ten pennies must and will come. He, the Protector of all, has to replenish the pocket of His devotee-only the giver must have absolute faith and indomitable courage.

Life is not and should not be one constant steady flow; and when you see dark clouds gathering and storms threatening to burst out you need not despair and leave the boat. Be steady at the helm of Truth and steer steadily on the path of safety which the *Rishi*-s had chalked out for us. Constantly referring to the compass of inner purity, self-ward gaze and go ahead...full steam, full speed. Keep smiling. Accept adverse criticism. Don't ever get perturbed. Words are but disturbances in the air created by merely wagging the tongue. If there is nothing true in the criticism, ignore it all as meaningless blabbering. If there is truth accept it with gratitude and bring about the necessary changes in you. Thus improve; come to shine more than ever before. Be grateful to all the creative critics all through your life.

This is your duty towards yourself; to live in self control, to eat and sleep properly, to exercise your body, to maintain a loving and peaceful attitude towards all, and to educate yourself more and more in your spiritual knowledge, so that you can serve well the people around you. Never give up self-study (*swaadhyaaya*), Worship the Lord. Meditate regularly. Be a fanatic in performing your daily "prayers" (*Anushtaana*). Never give it up for a day, whether you are traveling or sick.

This alone can bring sweetness in to your life. This alone is the path of Spirituality.

Whether a person dwells at home or in the forest, if one has dispassion (vairagya) one is a renunciate. One may puy on the orange robe go on mumbling the mantras, but one is no renunciate unless one has true dispassion. There seems to be nothing absurd in the idea of a householder (whether man or woman) immersing him or herself in divine thought even as the great rishis in their Himalayan ashrams did., provided he or she has the necessary discrimination (viveka) and dispassion.

The Vedic scriptures amply prove that in the past it was householders, more than renunciates, who worked in the field of philosphical thought. Indifference to worldly pleasures is the chief requisite for spiritual advancement.

Swami Tapovanam

The Stages of Life
Swami Tejomayananda

In the context of our present discussion, the meaning of *aashrama* is 'a stage in life.' Our Hindu scriptures describe four stages: the *brahmacharya aashrama* (the student's life), *grhastha aashrama* (the householder's life), *vaanaprastha aashrama* (The life of retirement or preparatory renunciation), and the *samnyaasa aashrama* (the renounced order of life). No real *vaanaprastha* stage exists today because no one knows what to do in their old age except retire, go to an old-age home, and watch television all day!

Our Hindu scriptures, however, are very scientific. Considering a human being's life to be 100 years maximum, the life span is divided roughly into four stages of twenty-five years, and so on. In fact, it is said that when you see the face of your grandson, you should retire for contemplation. Then there will be no generation gap problem! Remember, though one may criticize the older generation now, no matter how modern one thinks oneself to be at this moment, the next generation will also consider you an old and outdated person! Thus the scriptures say that before this happens, one should leave the house and prepare for renunciation. Then after *vaanaprastha*, one should take *sannyaasa*, the complete renunciation of all worldly affairs, and have total devotion to spiritual knowledge alone. This is the general scheme for the *varnaashrama*-s.

Prescribed Duties

For each *aashrama* or stage of life, particular duties are prescribed in the *shaastra*. We will see the first two :

Brahmacharya: The Student's Life. We read in the traditional accounts of how the student goes to live and study with the teacher performing *mundana* (shaving of the head), *homa* (sacrifice), and *havana* (daily sacrificial rituals). Though we may say that all this is irrelevant now, we should know that the underlying value holds as true today as it did then. The main principle enunciated for the disciple was: "If you are a *vidyaarthy* (one who is a seeker of knowledge alone), you must give up the idea of comforts." On the other hand, the scriptures say: "But if you are a seeker of comforts, then forget about knowledge," for it will not come to you.

In this so-called industrial civilization, the situation is as the latter statement indicates. Due to the smaller family units, the children get pampered with all kinds of comforts and possessions and fight each other for them. The children become glued to the television, and rather than becoming more intelligent, statistics show us that those who watch more television actually have lower I.Q.s, while those children who watch less television do better in their studies. The fact is that when a student chases after clothes, food, pleasures, and comforts, there is no time for study and concentration, and the mind becomes dissipated. The scriptures tell us that the first duty of the student is to be totally devoted to study and knowledge, to have devotion and respect for the teacher, as well as for the books of study. These days when students go out to sit on the lawn, if there is nothing else to sit on, they take out their books and sit on them! The student should also make no other demands on the family. If a students in the brahmacarya aashrama were also taught the eternal values of life (*sanaatana dharma*), which we have already discussed. They were taught the ultimate goal of life and how to prepare for it. Having learned the universal and general values of living, the students would then choose their own professions and train in that particular field--just as today the university students take general courses first, followed by specialized course in their chosen field.

Children of royal families, for instance, were taught political science, economics, warfare, and other related sciences.   Thereafter the students were ready for the nest stage of life, the householder's life. It is said in *Taittireeya Upanishad*: "Having given *dakshinaa* (gift) to your teacher, in the form of that which is most dear to him (and to you), do not cut off the line of descendants." (I;11) Out of gratitude we should give to the teacher *priya dhaana*, which means that which is not only dear to the teacher but also what is dear to us, because often we keep what is dear to us and give away only what we do not like!   After having taken permission from the teacher, one was free to enter into the householder's life.

Today we find these nobler ideas disappearing from the student's life, as the problem of dating is coming up more. Young Indians ask me angrily, "Swamiji, why do our parents prevent us from dating? We want to go to parties and other things." But then the very purpose of the student's life is defeated--the mind becomes completely distracted. Boy and girl meet each other and fall in love; they become infatuated with each other for some time, but later one of them goes away and the other is left shattered. Love is gone, study is gone, and knowledge is gone! I remind them that their whole life is before them to do all the things they want. Reserve the precious early years wholly for study and come to lead a fulfilling life. Thus, the students must devote their entire energy to educate themselves--not only to read and write, but also to lay a strong foundation for the moral, ethical, cultural, and spiritual aspects of life. Aside from academic training, our educational systems must give students a higher ideal for which to strive. The students must become the makers of their own destiny and of the nation's destiny also. This is their great responsibility.

The Householder's Life

Marriages are also of different types. When people ask me whether an arranged marriage or a love-marriage is best, I say, "A successful marriage is best!" Successful marriages have nothing to do with being arranged because there are examples of success and failure in both types of marriages. The main point is that there should be mutual love, respect, and readiness to sacrifice for each other. This is the ideal in mind, the marriage is successful;

but if each person in only demanding from the other there will always be a problem. There are many duties or *kartavya karma*-s prescribed for the householder's life. Though we cannot discuss them in detail here, one very important point should be brought out, which is given in the *shaastra*: "In those houses where the women are honored and respected, the gods dwell there. Where the women are not respected and honored, whatever one does is futile." In other words, if the lady of the house in unhappy or abused in any way, no work will bring fulfillment or prosperity to that house. Another verse says: "The husband must see that the wife is happy and the wife must see that the husband is happy. When both are making each other happy, there will be auspiciousness and welfare for all in that house." This is the ideal for the householder's life, and if this ideal is not held by both husband and wife, there will only be fighting between them; and when the children see this repeatedly, they will also fight. Such a household will be filled with violence. We see this catastrophe happening nowadays as the number of broken families, unwed mothers, single parent homes, and other such problems increase. These problems will also exist in the future as long as a person is only demanding from others.

Another instruction given to the householder concerns food: "Do not censure food, do not waste food, grow more food." Food also represents general wealth and prosperity: therefore the significance is that material prosperity should neither be criticized not wasted, but should be cultivated and shared with others, not used for that one household alone. In *Taittireeya Upanishad*, it is said: "Do not turn away anybody who seeks shelter and lodging. This is the vow. Let one, therefore, acquire much food by any means whatsoever". One should say, "Food is ready." If the food is prepared in the best manner, the food is given to him (the host) also in the best manner. If the food is prepared in a mediocre manner, food is also given to him (the host) in a mediocre manner. If food is prepared in the lowest manner, the same food is also given to him (the host). He who knows thus, will obtain all the rewards as mentioned above. (III:10)

In the midst of action, think of the soul. Sorrounded by wife, husband, and grandchildren, still think of the lord (*Paramatman*) with devout love. Think, constantly, of the power that activate you r hands and legs. Do not allow Yourself to be tempted by intoxicated wine. On the contrary, drink you fill of the nectar of life forever more and find everlasting bliss!

Swami Tapovanam

One who has no desire for enjoying the fleeting thrills of sense-gratifications (*bhoga-vaanccha - viyuktah*) is fit for *Samnyaas*. This state of mental detachment from sense-objects can come only to one who is deeply interested in, and therefore, constantly striving on the path of spiritual devlopment (*yoga*).

Swami Chinmayananda

It is all in the mind
Swami Chidananda

One of the ways *Maaya* plays its trick upon us is by making us believe that external factors are the cause of our bondage. We look around and say, "If I had more money, if I had a more understanding spouse, if my children were doing better at school, ... I would have been a happy person." In reality, however, even great disadvantages can be turned into wonderful spiritual challenges and then into beautiful opportunities for growth and deep satisfaction. What is needed is inner strength which comes from purity and maturity.

Who is a householder?

I would say - one who has strong attachments. Pujya Gurudev Swami Chinmayanandaji said, "He who depends on external situations for his happiness is a *samsaari*!" Conversely, one who has inner detachment is a *sannyaasi* (renunciant monk) irrespective of one's marital and economic status. It is the psychological phenomenon of 'I, me and my,' that makes anybody a householder. The Gita describes an advanced spiritualist as '*aniketa*,' meaning 'one without a house!'(XII.19).

As our spiritual awareness expands, we easily drop our notions of 'me and mine.' What is the difference then? While our mundane activities continue, to some extent at least, we are free of any mental preoccupation about our position and possessions.

The peace of the Self stays with us beyond the hour of formal meditation. We handle our responsibilities efficiently without any sense of personal insecurity. We do not waste our energy on unnecessary thought, word or deed. Do we become insensitive? No. On the contrary, we are more caring than ever. Instead of just trying to please everybody and yield to emotionalism, we pay keen attention to the root cause of problems - of others or of ourselves. The result is that our actions are very beneficial in the long range. In the *Adhyaatma Raamaayana,* Vibhishana praises Lord Sri Rama as *'anaadi grihastha'* i.e. a householder from beginningless time (VI.iii.17). Yes,God runs the largest household, for all creation is His family! Saints around whom large ashrams grow are in almost the same boat. There are endless causes for getting disturbed if we identify ourselves with the ups and downs around us.

Spirituality teaches us to raise our head above all trifles of daily life. We are fine, no matter what. This is not shutting our eyes to imperfections. It is learning to be objective,attentive and truly effective. Our self-worth should not be at the mercy of words or actions of other people. We notice there are problems that need to be solved. We do not allow them to sweep us off our feet.Scriptural study and meditation enable us to maintain inner equilibrium and deal with issues with a sense of direction based on correct principles of human well-being.

Detachment and self-control

All attachment begins with our attachment to our own body. In that sense, everyone of us is a householder with one spouse and ten children right away! Mind is the spouse and the ten senses are the children. The outer spouse and kids are thus our extended family. Incidentally, what is the plural of 'spouse?' Somewhere once, my audience confused me by saying it is like the word mouse. Spouse becomes spice! The body, the mind and the intellect (BMI) are therefore our immediate family. Exercise, Meditation and Study (XMS) on a regular basis keep the BMI in fine shape. A minimum of 20 minutes daily of each of these three disciplines leads to what I call as the 20/20/20 program which might remind you of the popular 20/20 program on a TV channel in North America.

Detachment begins with right understanding. Knowing ourselves better, we stop the two errors that cause all entanglements. One, over-indulgence and second, denial of genuine needs. Mere appeasement of people on one hand, and ideo-logical conceptions on the other lead us away from being true to ourselves. People-pleasers as well as unprepared ascetics suffer unnecessarily. We need to look within and position ourselves correctly with respect to all our activities. The Gita advises moderation in all departments of our daily life such as food, sleep and movements (VI.17). 'Look before you leap!' goes the old saying. Speech is another important area where daily life presents numerous opportunities for discreet use of the faculty.

Self-control born of right understanding resolves very many conflicts of a householder's life. Responsibilities strain us and we want to retire into solitude. Sri Ramana Maharshi says, 'Retirement means abidance in the Self' (Talks p.206). He clarifies that one otherwise leaves one set of surroundings and gets entangled in another set. One might leave the concrete world and get involved in a mental world! Be where you are and practice spiritual disciplines. Somebody asked the Maharshi why then he had left home. He answered that it had been his *praarabdha*! (*Praarabdha* means the destined result of one's past actions.) (Talks, p.209) The essence of freedom therefore has nothing to do with what we are in our outer life. Inner change gives us peace and that is possible in the so-called householder's life too. Popular religion, lacking in precision, seems to equate family life with worldliness and a monk's life with spirituality. These equations are an oversimplification of truth and are therefore not at all dependable.

Finally, the key to spiritual growth is one's own earnest self-application to the voice of God that is within one's own heart. In sincere introspection and self-enquiry, the ego in us melts and we find the true Self in us which is ever free.

Multiplicity of worldly concerns binds down a
Sanyasin as much as any householder.
Swami Chinmayananda

Begin with yourself
Swami Ishwarananda

Culture of a society rests in the conduct of the householders. Family culture has become an important issue of today's world. In fact, a society by itself is one big family. Each member of the society is equally responsible for the total well-being of the society and a householder is, therefore the true representative of the culture of the society. In the past, many thinkers have dedicated their life in restructuring the value system in the society, for the total harmony and prosperity of the society of their times.

In the ancient Tamil literature, *Thirukkural* is considered as the most practical scripture, written by *Thiruvalluvar,* a noble householder, to guide men and women of all walks of life. He had dedicated his life in the education of social culture. We shall reflect upon a few of his ideas about householders' life:

Love and concern

Love and concern for all beings is the life of a householder. The absence of which is mere existence of skin covering the bones. (80)

It is not mere living together that makes a family. It is love and concern for each other which brings significant harmony and integrity to the family life. As a householder one has to cultivate love, instead of attachment, for his kith and kin. Let him constantly remember that it is Lord himself who is now his own wife and children. Let him expand this pure love to all beings. Swami Vivekananda said, "Let him see God in that which is dear to him. This is the beginning. Let him slowly expand his vision to embrace one and all in that pure love".

One who has not found abundance of love in his bosom cannot have the real 'concern for others'. It is an expression of fullness. The Bhagavad Gita says, 'O Arjuna, he is regarded as the integrated soul (*yogin*) who sees equality everywhere, be it a pleasure or pain, through the sameness of the Self" (V1.32). Normally we get concerned in a situation only if we are to benefit by our involvement. Whereas a highly evolved soul has a natural tendency to help others, even if he has nothing to gain from that very act. In Vivekachoodamani, Sri Shankaracharya refers such a nature of an evolved soul as *para-shrama-apanoda-pravanam* (inclination to remove the troubles of others) (38). Every householder should therefore, strive to inculcate this quality ,even a little measure in his daily life.

- *Have the feeling of the presence of God in all - to begin with, in near and dear ones*
- *Practice one simple act of concern in daily life; it is an offering to God.*

Patience leads to peace

One (a householder) who can bear the insults of others with patience is as pure as a renunciate monk.(159)

Life is never a smooth flow of events and situations. Every twist and turn in life provides us an opportunity to learn and evolve. A householder can evolve to be a spiritual aspirant only if he can practice the quality of patience in the midst of pressing situations. Peace is the direct result of patience coupled with wisdom. The Bhagavad Gita says, " He who is able to withstand (with patience) the impulse born of desire and anger while still living (in this world), before the fall of the body, is an integrated soul (*yogin*) and a happy man" (V.23).We can go to further extent and say, 'Positive patience is the expression of maturity; it is the sign of wisdom'.

- *Listen to others with patience without any particular motive to take advantage of the situation*
- *Engage in a sincere attempt to find peace in simple acts of patience in daily life*

Right knowledge - Right Perception

Mere shaving of head and growing a long beard (external signs of renunciation) are not necessary if one has given up sinful deeds in the world..(280)

According to many thinkers, living with ethical and moral values as a householder is more difficult than a living as a renunciate monk. It may be true. A true renunciate has nothing to gain from the world and hence his interactions with the world are minimum. Whereas a householder who is in the midst of fulfilling his worldly duties and also striving to lead a pure life will have to face different challenges both in domestic and social life. Finding a true balance in various situations is the test of spiritual progress. Sri Gandhiji once observed: 'Man's serenity of mind can be tested only in the world of men, not in the solitary heights of Himalayas!'

According to Pujya Gurudev Swami Chinmaya-nanda, 'Sin is not in action; it is in reaction'. Changing our attitudes and changing our perception of life are the essential teachings of Bhagavad Gita. And that is the sure way to bring real meaning to our life. Sinful reactions are due to absence of right thinking. Knowledge plays a vital role in proper thinking and management of emotions.

No doubt, absence of knowledge is ignorance but greater is the misery of ignorance for a person who knows what to do and yet ignores them. Mere reading of religious books and visit to holy shrines, by themselves do not make one, spiritually evolved. It is the silent practice of values in daily life, which, over a period of time fructifies into spiritual maturity.

- *Study and contemplation of the messages of Bhagavad Gita and similar scriptures, must be a part of our daily life*

- *Daily spiritual practices like worship, prayer and meditation help us act and react with a positive mind.*

Such inspiring guidance from ancient masters are the treasures of Hindu Culture. May we strive to evolve as fit instruments of their grace!

There is nothing wrong if a householder, residing in his own house, tries to realize Brahman even as a renunciate does in the forest. People in all stages of life are entitled to the enjoyment of spiritual bliss. It is their birthright. Spiritual realization is not impracticable even in the midst of worldly activities, provided one has the necessary mental strength.

No one steeped in sensuous pleasures can ever find abidance in Brahman. Can a lotus ever grow on rocks or hair on tortoise shells ?

Do not give up spiritual exercises until you experience peace, the ineffable, interminable peace that characterizes liberation, through external activities. It is not merely putting an end to sorrows; it is not merely experiencing joys; it is the experience of a state of Bliss transcending all other experiences.

Swami Tapovanam

Thus spake *Swami Chinmayananda*............

To receive love from outside us is to be ever indebted to the world around

Let your tongue remain silent; let your hands and legs serve. Let your heart flood the atmosphere with love. You will then be creating an enchanting magic around you, that others, however bad they may be, cannot but reciprocate your love to you

To give love is to expand. Thereafter the lover functions from two centers - one from within himself and another from the beloved, a center outside himself.

To love others has been the function of the greatest devotees. To give love to others is the privilege of the few. The large majority of creatures are beggars of love. They demand love. They expect to receive love.

To give love we must become independent in ourselves and be a pillar in life for others to hold on to us. Such an individual, who needs no crutches for his own existence, alone can have the power to give love. All others are receivers of love.

One who knows how to give love is a living god upon earth. To gain this mastery is the highest achievement in life.

Love is the very basis of Hinduism. If you know how to love you are a Hindu. All great people have become great because of their love for others. They gained greatness because they learnt to love.

Any little *seva* to others, at any time, is a glorious chance that the Lord has given to us to serve Him! Make use of every such chance.

Love is not a mere superficial emotion, it is a gracious expression of the mind when it discovers its total identity with the things and beings around. This total love can spring in the mind only when it has fully evolved and has become strengthened with wisdom.

In ardent faith, with true and deep devotion, and with the mind not running to the sense objects, if we can turn our attention for a few moments a day to call out to Him, it will be the most effective prayer.

Think well before you undertake any work. Do not plunge into work in a hasty and hurried manner and then repent for having done so. Even if you meet with failure in work that you undertook after much planning, it does not matter. You will not feel unhappy about your failure in that attempt, for you will have a sense of satisfaction in having done your best.